A Pillar Box Red Publication

© 2014. Published by Pillar Box Red Publishing Ltd. Printed in the EU.

ISBN: 978-1-907823-52-7

Photographs © Corbis and Shutterstock.com

5 SECONDS OF SUMMER

A 2015 ANNUAL

Written by Helen Selby
Designed by Chris Dalrymple

CONTENTS

THE STORY SO FAR...

First there was one, then there were three, next there were four... and BOOM! 5 Seconds of Summer were born. Starting out by posting covers of songs on YouTube in 2011, these four guys have been propelling their way to super stardom ever since.

So, allow us to introduce... Luke Hemmings (lead vocals, guitar), Michael Clifford (guitar, vocals), Calum Hood (bass guitar, vocals) and Ashton Irwin (drums, vocals). The boys got together in Sydney, Australia. They officially class themselves as a rock band, rather than a boy band. Why? They write their own songs and play their own instruments... awesome! Ashton was the last to join the band, becoming the force that drove them towards fame. Well, they wouldn't be the same without him!

Before officially becoming a band, Luke, Michael and Calum were friends who attended Norwest Christian College in Riverstone, Sydney. Luke began posting cover songs on his YouTube account. The first one? A cover of Mike Posner's *Please Don't Go*, which was posted on 3rd February, 2011. The others joined him for cover after cover, with Ashton finally joining in December 2011, completing the amazing line up we see today. Unsurprisingly, 5 Seconds of Summer were an instant hit online, with views totting up daily.

The guys bonded more and more as they performed gigs in local pubs, covering songs by old school punk bands such as Blink-182. They had a great time, but it wasn't exactly the stuff dreams are made of. However, in November 2012, after their fame online had grown to enormous heights, 5 Seconds of Summer released *Out Of My Limit*, their very first single. It was viewed over 100,000 times in just 24 hours! Just a month later, things really began to change for the foursome. A song-writing trip to London was a total game-changer. The guys wrote songs with the likes of Nick Hodgson from Kaiser Chiefs, Roy Stride from Scouting for Girls, James Bourne from Busted and the boys from McFly. They also worked with well-known producers and song-writers like Jamie Scott (who has worked with One Direction), Jake Gosling (who has also worked with One Direction as well as Ed Sheeran) and Steve Robson (who has worked with One Direction too, plus Olly Murs). Not bad!

Now, by this time, 5 Seconds of Summer were getting more and more attention on an international level. One Direction spotted their cover of *Teenage Dirtbag* online, which prompted none other than Louis Tomlinson to send a message into the Twittersphere stating: "Been a fan of this band for a while, everyone get behind them" with a link to their original song, *Gotta Get Out*. Over 70,000 retweets later, the boys began fast-tracking their way to international stardom. They got their first break by supporting American pop rock band Hot Chelle Rae on a tour of Australia, causing their fan base to grow even more. With a new air of confidence, it was time to embark on their own tour of their home country.

Of course, the real turning point came when the boys were offered the chance to support One Direction on their worldwide Take Me Home Tour. This was announced in February 2013. 5 Seconds of Summer were already doing very well in Australia by this point, but decided it would be crazy to turn down such an awesome opportunity. Er, duh! Now One Direction and 5 Seconds of Summer are best pals, despite their musical styles differing slightly (5 Seconds of Summer are definitely a little more punk rocky). 5 Seconds of Summer's own army of fans has since grown, making them stars in their own right. Their first EP, *She Looks So Perfect*, debuted at number two in the US and number one in over 45 countries... wow! It seems they've already come a huge way since the days of YouTube covers, and we're sure there's still so much more to come!

So, what next? Sold out tours? Exciting adventures? World domination? Who knows? That was only the story so far...

LIVE ON STAGE

5 Seconds of Summer perform to a sold out hysterical, screaming, fainting audience at the Manchester Ritz, February 2014.

5 Seconds of Summer perform on stage during a meeting with fans in Madrid, Spain, April 2014.

ROYAL OAK

AEGLIVE
PRESENTS

SOLD
OUT

5 SECONDS
OF SUMMER

FRI 7 PM DRS

ROMTLIVECOM

Live at the Royal Oak Music Theatre, Michigan, USA, April 2014.

Fans wait for 5 Seconds of Summer to take to the stage at the Sound Academy in Toronto, Canada, April 2014.

5 Seconds of Summer perform "She Looks So Perfect" at the 2014 Billboard Music Awards in Las Vegas, USA, May 2014.

Performing at the Perth Convention and Exhibition Centre in Perth, Western Australia, May 2014.

Performing on 'Voice of Italy' in Milan, Italy, June 2014.

In concert at Esprit Arena in Dusseldorf, Germany, July 2014.

DID YOU KNOW?

The 5 Seconds of Summer tour bus is called Gus, and it's more like a hotel than a bus! He also has more than 20,000 followers (and counting) on Twitter!

Work started on the 5 Seconds of Summer debut album way back in December 2012.

Good Girls was co-written by Roy from Scouting For Girls!

BROMANCE

According to Luke, the band were originally going to be called 'Bromance'! Yikes.

GUS

The band became the fourth Australian band to have a UK number one single. They were the first to do so in 14 years. Nice work boys!

LUKE HEMMINGS

Full Name: Luke Robert Hemmings

Date of Birth: 16th July 1996

Star Sign: Cancer

Place of Birth: Sydney, Australia

Relationship Status: Single

Band Position: Guitarist and lead vocalist.

Superhero Alter Ego: Doctor Fluke

Mum and Dad: Liz and Andrew.

Siblings: Two brothers called Ben and Jack.

Pets: A dog called Molly.

Looks: Lower lip piercing, blonde hair and blue eyes.

Secret Obsession: He supports the Sydney Swans in the Australian Football League.

Education: Attended Norwest Christian College.

Hidden Talents: Snowboarding. Cool!

Favourite Colour: Blue

Favourite Animal: Penguin

Celebrity Crush: Mila Kunis

Favourite Singer: Josh Ramsay

Favourite Food: Pizza

Random Fact: He is an uncle! Luke's niece is called Zoe.

MICHAEL CLIFFORD

Full Name: Michael Gordon Clifford

Date of Birth: 20th November 1995

Star Sign: Scorpio

Place of Birth: Sydney, Australia

Relationship Status: Single

Band Position: Guitarist and vocalist.

Superhero Alter Ego: Mike-Ro-Wave (ha ha)

Mum: Karen

Siblings: He's an only child.

Pets: He once had a little Siamese kitten called Teddy... aww!

Looks: Green eyes and naturally blonde hair, but he likes to experiment with the dye! So far Michael's hair has been blonde, black, blue, pink, white, black and red, black and purple, black with a blue stripe, dark brown and 'reverse skunk'. Hair-raising stuff!

Secret Obsession: He loves gaming.

Favourite Song: He wishes he had written *Miss You* by Blink-182.

Education: Attended Norwest Christian College.

Favourite Colour: Blue

Favourite Movies: Forrest Gump and The Pursuit Of Happyness.

Celebrity Crush: Camila Cabello

Favourite Band: All Time Low

Favourite Food: He loves Nandos!

Random Fact: He is part English, part Scottish, part Irish, part German and part Australian.

CALUM HOOD

Full Name: Calum Thomas Hood

Date of Birth: 25th January 1996

Star Sign: Aquarius

Place of Birth: Sydney, Australia. By blood, he's half Kiwi and half Scottish.

Relationship Status: Single

Band Position: Bassist

Superhero Alter Ego: Cal Pal

Mum and Dad: Joy and David.

Siblings: Mali

Favourite Animal: Dog

Looks: Dark hair and deep brown eyes.

Secret Obsession: Rumour has it Calum is a great salsa dancer!

Favourite Song: Just like Michael, he wishes he had written *Miss You* by Blink-182!

Education: Attended Norwest Christian College.

Hidden Talents: Calum was about to embark on a career in professional football before the band took off.

Favourite Colour: Baby blue

Favourite Childhood Movie: *Monsters Inc.*

Celebrity Crush: Katy Perry

Favourite Food: Pizza

Random Fact: He supports Liverpool FC!

ASHTON IRWIN

Full Name: Ashton Fletcher Irwin

Date of Birth: 7th July 1994

Star Sign: Cancer

Place of Birth: Hornsby, Australia

Relationship Status: Single

Band Position: Drummer

Superhero Alter Ego: Smash

Mum: Anne-Marie

Siblings: Harry and Lauren.

Pets: A dog called Indie.

Looks: Wavy blondish-brown hair, cute dimples and hazel brown eyes.

Secret Obsession: He's a big fan of Dragon Ball Z.

Education: Attended Richmond High School.

Hidden Talents: Ash can also play the saxophone, piano and guitar.

Favourite Colour: Red

Favourite Animal: Dog

Celebrity Crushes: Hayley Williams and Jade from Little Mix.

Favourite Singer: James Morrison

Favourite Food: Spaghetti

Random Fact: He was the last to join the band.

21

SPOT THE DIFFERENCE

Ooer, here comes double trouble! Well, octuplet trouble if you want to get technical. Reckon you know enough about the boys to detect a mile away when something's not quite right? Prove it! Look closely at these pictures and see if you can spot all nine differences. Take as long as you need, but if you can do it in five seconds, kudos!

You can find the answers on page 60.

DID YOU KNOW?

When the band first got together, Ashton used to drive them to and from gigs and rehearsals. Why? He was the only one that could drive!

Apparently, Ashton snores a lot. Ha ha!

ZZZZ

Luke can get quite bad nerves before heading on stage. Don't worry Luke! We love you!

Calum's sister, Mali Koa Hood, competed on The Voice Australia. Check out the video online and see if you can spot a baby-faced Calum!

Luke has a massive fluffy penguin toy that hangs around on the tour bus. How adorable!

THE BEST 5 SECONDS OF SUMMER QUIZ... EVER!

So, like to think of yourself as 5 Seconds of Summer's biggest fan? This is the ultimate test of how well you know the boys! Oh, by the way, peeking at the answers is not allowed! (Psst, they're on page 60!)

1 In which year did the band get together?

2 What was the first cover song that Luke posted on YouTube?

3 Which one of the boys was the only one not to attend Norwest Christian College?

4 What type of animal is Ketchup?

5 Why did Luke once eat seventeen whole bowls of ice-cream in a row?

6 Which one of the boys is a bit obsessed with *Pokémon*?

7 Which National Rugby League team does Luke support?

8 Which food product do the guys always have a jar of, no matter where they are in the world?

9 The guys collaborated with Benji and Joel Madden during the making of their debut album. Can you name which band those guys are from?

10 In the video for *Don't Stop*, the lads transform into superheroes. Which one has a bright green and yellow costume?

11 Which animal does Luke refer to himself as in his Instagram name?

12 Which band member has a Scottish dad?

13 What is Michael's natural hair colour?

14 What was the name of the 2013 One Direction tour that the boys were the support act for?

15 In what year did the boys win the gong for Best Breakthrough Band at the MTV Awards?

16 Which band member almost became a professional footballer?

17 What's the longest song on the album, *5 Seconds of Summer*?

18 Fill in the gap to complete the sentence. 5 Seconds of Summer are a _____ band.

19 Which member admitted via Twitter to being guilty of wearing Crocs?

20 Which one of the lads proudly posted a pic of himself hanging out with Rolling Stones rocker Ronnie Wood on his Instagram?

TWEET TWEET!

Don't you just love the power of Twitter? You can take a sneaky peak into the lives of 5 Seconds of Summer whenever you fancy it. In fact, let's do it now! Here's a collection of some of the most random, hilarious and interesting tweets from the band. Don't forget to go follow them online at... @Calum5SOS, @Luke5SOS, @Ashton5SOS and @Michael5SOS!

Calum Hood @Calum5SOS
I love and appreciate every single poster, letter and gift you guys have for us. #BIGLOVEx

Ashton Irwin @Ashton5SOS
I ate a steak for breakfast...I am a dinosaur

Luke Hemmings @Luke5SOS
Excuse me waiter, can I have a hug?

Luke Hemmings @Luke5SOS
London you're crazy, and I like that

Michael Clifford @Michael5SOS
Bed is the best

Ashton Irwin @Ashton5SOS
Can't believe with 3 dorks I met 3 and a half years ago, we managed to overcome so much, and make our first ever album, thanks to you guys

Michael Clifford @Michael5SOS
Will never understand how people eat tomatoes.. goodnight

Calum Hood @Calum5SOS
Ya know when something's not right in a song but you don't know what to change it to?

Luke Hemmings @Luke5SOS
I would get up early, but that would also involve me being on time for something

Calum Hood @Calum5SOS
GRAB YOUR BANDANAS, DYE YOUR HAIR AND GET READY TO ROCK OUT!

Ashton Irwin @Ashton5SOS
A 14 year old kid was teasing me at the airport cause I was air drumming, I felt like I was at school all over again

Michael Clifford @Michael5SOS

Imagine if the entire world was populated with kittens, instead of 6 billion humans there were 6 billion kittens #weneedcatnip

Calum Hood @Calum5SOS

Hotels should really have petting zoos

Ashton Irwin @Ashton5SOS

I just want people to sing our songs at the top of their lungs in cars, malls, bus stops, anywhere & everywhere

Luke Hemmings @Luke5SOS

The moment that you realize not everyone is going to like you, it's a nice one.

Calum Hood @Calum5SOS

When my hair gets too long it starts to look like a mini afro.

Ashton Irwin @Ashton5SOS

Got spaghetti on my chin

Michael Clifford @Michael5SOS

If you like our band I probably like you more then Luke does

Luke Hemmings @Luke5SOS

I feel sorry for people who don't have a favourite band :) I love bands

Ashton Irwin @Ashton5SOS

Everyone has a scooter here, I want a scooter

Calum Hood @Calum5SOS

There's only so much pasta a man can eat

Michael Clifford @Michael5SOS

Just watched a chick flick with Luke, now we need to do something manly like push ups or eat steak

Michael Clifford @Michael5SOS

Nothin beats heated floors EVER

Luke Hemmings @Luke5SOS

In negative news I had a bad milkshake

THE PERFECT PLAYLIST

What would you hear blasting from the boys' headphones if you were sat behind them on the bus? Here, Ashton shares a collection of music 5 Seconds of Summer love, with three of the bands that inspired them to get into the music biz. Press play!

GREENDAY

Who? An awesome punk rock band that got together way back in 1987.

Tell me more! These guys helped punk hit the mainstream, they've been a huge influence on 5 Seconds of Summer! Check out their classic album, *Dookie*.

What Ashton said: "I look up to guys like Tré Cool (Green Day drummer) in my drumming." (hmv.com)

PARAMORE

Who? An alternative rock band hailing from America.

Tell me more! They're fronted by Hayley Williams, the girl with a powerful voice and bright orange hair.

What Ashton said: "My favourite band, musically and live, is Paramore – I think they're incredible. Their song writing is incredible and as the drummer of this band, the drums on the new record were just amazing."
(alterthepress.com)

ALL TIME LOW

Who? An American pop punk band who collaborated with 5 Seconds of Summer on their album.

Tell me more! This band got together in high school and started out by covering songs by their favourite bands. Hmm... have we heard this story somewhere before?

What Ashton said: "Most of all, I think we look up to All Time Low, they've got this perfect mix of pop and rock."
(hmv.com)

Who else is on the 5 Seconds of Summer's playlist?

BIFFY CLYRO

FOO FIGHTERS

MY CHEMICAL ROMANCE

JOHN MAYER

BLINK-182

SUM 41

LINKIN PARK

IMAGINE DRAGONS

JIMMY EAT WORLD

JAMES MORRISON

NIRVANA

Why not list your fave artists too?

_____

_____

_____

_____

_____

_____

_____

_____

_____

_____

_____

_____

WORD UP!

```
K  P  U  N  K  R  P  K  L  E  X  T
B  T  B  T  A  K  Q  A  T  M  P  H
M  V  R  T  X  R  T  I  Z  T  I  V
W  I  I  U  E  K  M  L  Y  Y  H  O
Z  U  K  M  O  E  D  A  L  L  S  C
G  B  M  E  G  T  G  R  F  Q  D  A
M  U  A  E  R  Q  J  T  X  H  N  L
S  J  V  S  M  O  R  S  P  T  E  S
J  K  V  D  S  O  W  U  Z  W  I  B
K  F  R  A  C  S  D  A  E  H  R  R
Z  M  T  K  X  H  W  D  V  R  F  M
K  N  D  R  U  M  S  M  N  E  K  X
```

There are twelve words hidden in this wordsearch – how many can you find? Look closely! The words could go up, down, left, right, horizontally and diagonally!

Australia   **Drums**   **Headscarf**

Vocals   **Guitar**   **Bass**

Rock   **Summer**

Tour   **Friendship**

Vegemite

Punk

BONUS! One of the boys is in there too! Here's a hint: he may be hiding in there as his super alter-ego...

ALL MUDDLED UP!

We know the 5 Seconds of Summer lads are great with words, just look at their lyrics! Do you think you're just as good though? See how quickly you can unmuddle these song titles...

1. Pond tots

2. Shriveling leaf oaf

3. Drools gig

4. Anyhow log me

5. Freckles posh toe so

TRUE OR FALSE?

There are a lot of crazy rumours out there in celebrity land! Do you know enough about 5 Seconds of Summer to separate the fact from the fiction?

1. The band shot to fame when Zayn Malik tweeted about one of their songs.

2. Michael loves the Disney movie, *Camp Rock*.

3. Ashton is a huge fan of John Mayer.

4. Calum and Luke are cousins.

5. The band were originally going to be called '5 Seconds of Winter'.

Answers on page 60/61.

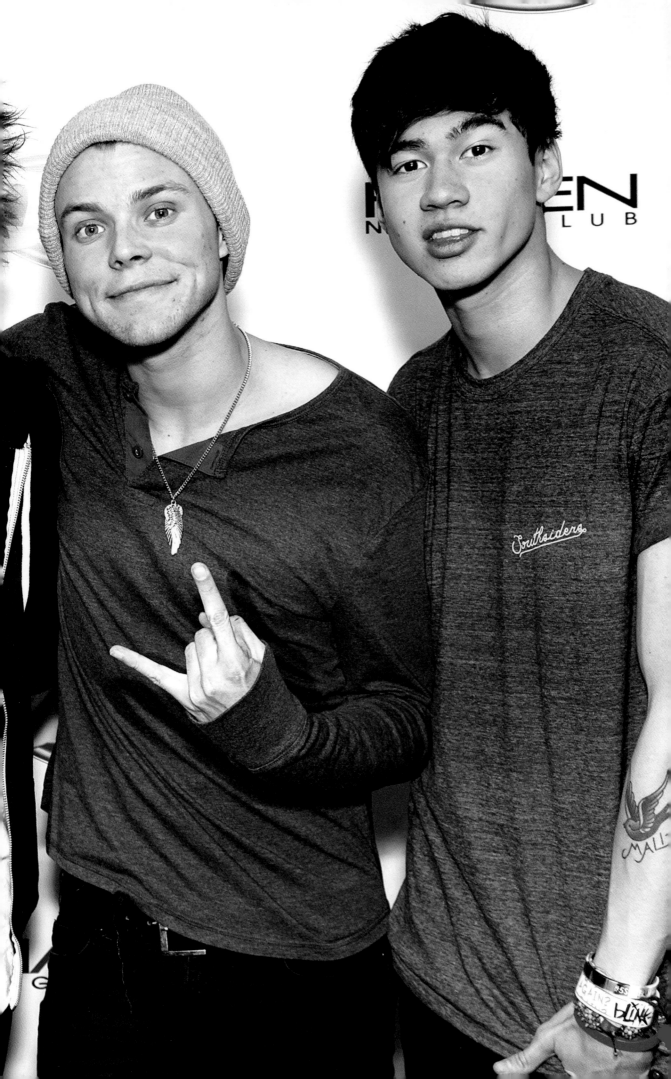

5 SECONDS OF STYLE!

Take a few cups of leather, add a spoonful of studs, mix in a dash of plaid and blend with a whole lot of rock and roll. What do you get? 5 Seconds of Summer of course! It can't be denied that each of the 5 Seconds of Summer lads has a unique sense of style that makes any magazine cover look good. They've spawned a whole new generation of rock chicks and punk guys who can't help model outfits on them. Here are just three of the coolest trademarks the guys have been sporting lately... which is your fave?

GRUNGY SHIRTS

Whether it's plaid, denim or cotton, a loose shirt chucked on over a T-shirt or vest has become a 5 Seconds of Summer fashion staple. Michael even rips the sleeves off his every now and again for a totally unique style! The guys tend to rock this look with those classic skinny jeans, but if it's a little chilly outside, out come the leather jackets!

SKINNY JEANS

A classic for any rock boy! You need serious swagger to pull a pair of these off, not to mention a great understanding of accessories. Worn on their own? Normal joe. Adorn them with chains, scarves and ripped knees and you have yourself a rock god! Luke has been known to add a cheeky touch to the trend with a bright green pair.

ROCK TEES

Any true 5 Seconds of Summer fan knows how much the boys appreciate the fathers of punk and rock. They regularly pay homage to their musical inspirations by wearing band T-shirts of Nirvana, Joy Division, Def Leppard, The Rolling Stones, Queen, AC/DC, Green Day and loads more. Something even cooler? Cartoon tees! We know Ashton is partial to a My Little Pony motif or two...

BAND

HOW CAN YOU GET THE LOOK?

GUYS!

Skinny jeans are your new best friend. Wear a black pair with a baggy vest of your favourite band (er, 5 Seconds of Summer, surely). Chuck on a loose denim shirt and add a long necklace for quirky cool. Feeling brave? Hello lip ring! Don't forget to add a cheeky grin...

GIRLS!

It's easy. Team a pair of ripped denim shorts with a 5 Seconds of Summer tee and some chunky boots. Finish the look off with a plaid shirt as a cover up. If it gets too warm, tie it around your waist! You'll look so perfect standing there...

WHY YOU LOVE 5 SECONDS OF SUMMER...

This is a keepsake page for true fans. Put a tick next to the answers you agree with, and don't forget to fill in your own, too! There's no right or wrong here, this is just a chance for you to write down what really makes you smile about 5 Seconds of Summer!

I first knew I liked 5 Seconds of Summer when...

☐ My friend sent me a link to one of their videos.

☐ I saw a picture of them in my fave magazine.

☐ I heard they were supporting One Direction!

☐ ....
....
....

I love singing along to their songs because...

☐ They're musically awesome.

☐ Their voices are amazing!

☐ I know all the words, off by heart!

☐ ....
....
....

If I ever got the chance to see them live, I'd...

☐ Try and get right to the front!

☐ Think I was dreaming!

☐ Make sure my best friends came with me!

☐ ....
....
....

I think the thing I like most about the band is...

☐ The fact that they're so talented.

☐ The way they dress.

☐ Their humour! They're absolutely hilarious.

☐ ....
....
....

If I ever met them in person, I would probably...

☐ Scream! Then flail. Then scream some more!

☐ Tell them how talented they are.

☐ Faint!

☐ ....
....
....

If I could work with the band, I would be...

☐ An awesome backing singer!

☐ A fantastic stylist.

☐ The best tour bus driver in the world!

☐ ....
....
....

Something I would do to make the guys laugh is ....
....
....

If I got to meet any of their mums, I would say..
....

My favourite member of the band is ...., because...
....
....

If I could only listen to one song by 5 Seconds of Summer for the rest of my life, I would

have to choose..

STARS IN THEIR EYES...

Do you know what your star sign says about you? When you were born can reveal a lot about your personality. We're going to unearth what 5 Seconds of Summer's signs say about them. Thank your lucky stars!

CANCER

LUKE AND ASHTON: CANCER

The Cancer-born are home-loving characters who love being around family in familiar surroundings. However, although they're very domestic, they are also very sociable and like to hang out in big groups of people. They're very nurturing souls who empathise well with people. They always make it their aim to make other people happy... aww! As a result of being so emotionally attached to places and people, Cancers are very in touch with their feelings. This can sometimes lead to grumpiness and mood swings – oh dear. On the plus side, Cancers always have lots of friends who they genuinely care about. That explains Luke and Ashton's love for their fans then! Although Cancers like these guys do love to please others, they also like to get their own way, and if they can't, they sulk. Cheer up boys! People under this sign also tend to be quite impulsive, meaning they can sometimes make crazy decisions without really thinking things through. Well, if crazy decision-making is what caused the birth of 5 Seconds of Summer, we're all for it!

MICHAEL: SCORPIO

SCORPIO

Scorpios are loving, caring and passionate about what they do. They are also very loyal people. Befriend a Scorpio and you've got yourself a pal for life - but this can sometimes mean they're a little possessive! One of the things Scorpios are great at is being creative and unique – that explains Michael's hair then! When they're not being all quirky, though, they're actually very resourceful and are great at solving problems. This can be great in situations with lots of people – if there's a confrontation, Scorpios are great at being the voice of reason and restoring order. People with this sign don't tend to be quite as sociable as others though, and they enjoy their independence. They're also very driven, and can become very committed to just about anything they set their mind to! The down side of this is that they tend to be rather competitive, and will always strive to be the best. A lot of Scorpios tend to be a little mysterious too, and don't like to give too much away about their personality. Something else to note about Scorpios is their very strange sense of humour... hmm, ring any bells?

AQUARIUS

CALUM: AQUARIUS

Aquarian guys are social butterflies that ooze confidence. They're very polite and respectful of other people, but they do have a cheeky rebellious streak – sounds like Calum! Aquarians are also very curious types who like to be kept in the loop and always know what's going on around them. This is usually easy though, as they're witty and sociable – so they're loads of fun to be around! People with this star sign are often a very good judge of character too. It can take a while to get close to them, but once they've sussed you out and decided to be friends with you, they'll do absolutely anything for you. Aquarians are always on a mission to make things better and improve the world where they can – which explains their high likeability factor. They're peacekeepers who also happen to be very strong-willed. Routine bores Aquarians like Calum, and they're always on the lookout for a new adventure. We'd say being a member of one of the coolest rock bands around is a good place to start!

IS IT WRITTEN IN THE STARS?

Reckon you and the guys could be best mates? Check out which signs they're compatible with to see how well you'd get on!

 **Luke and Ashton: Cancer – Compatible with Scorpio and Pisces.**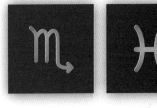

 **Michael: Scorpio – Compatible with Cancer and Pisces.**

 **Calum: Aquarius – Compatible with Gemini and Libra.**

DID YOU KNOW?

All four members of the band like to clean their teeth before going on stage. How very hygienic! Say cheese...

The boys all love the English accent! Who doesn't!?

Rumour has it that *Out Of My Limit* was originally called *Over The Limit*, but the band changed it so it wouldn't seem like it was about alcohol! Very sensible lads.

They have huge love for their fans and show their appreciation by always posing for photos and retweeting them when they can.

Michael had never been to a concert before one of his own. That's actually pretty cool!

HE SAID WHAT!?

Check out some of the best quotes from our favourite Aussies.

On the industry...
"It isn't the 1980s anymore, you can't be a mysterious dude and a huge rock star, people want real people." - Ashton
(hmv.com)

On each other...
"Luke would be the shy one; Ashton is the talker and the funny one; Michael is the wild one... and I'm just the chill dude." – Calum
(seventeen.com)

On their shows...
"We like our shows to be a big party vibe y'know? We want it to be an amazing experience." - Luke
(alterthepress.com)

On their sound...
"Usually live, our songs are a bit more bare, stripped back to drums, guitars, bass and vocals with such a little bit of track in there. But we can play without it, we've played arenas without it." – Michael
(hmv.com)

On other people...
"I'm a big fan of character, something individual in a person is amazing!" - Ashton
(alterthepress.com)

On stereotyping...
"We get the boyband tag a lot, we don't try and fight it, but it doesn't really fit." - Luke
(hmv.com)

On fame...
"It's crazy for us, but we're so grateful for every single person that supported us — not many people where we live get this kind of opportunity to do what they love." - Calum
(seventeen.com)

On staying in control...
"When we see negative comments, they genuinely get us down, we want fans to understand what decisions we make." - Ashton
(hmv.com)

On being recognised...
"When I had bright pink hair there was literally no hiding." - Michael
(hmv.com)

On touring...
"I don't think we can really prepare for that. We're pretty scared, but I think we're kind of hiding it at the moment." - Calum
(seventeen.com)

On the way they live...
"Obviously we know that not everyone's going to like every decision we make, but our fans know we do things for the right reasons." - Luke
(hmv.com)

And Mikey just being Mikey...
"I'm into socks that aren't odd. It's a good day if you're not wearing odd socks." - Michael
(popcrush.com)

WHICH 5 SECONDS OF SUMMER MEMBER ARE YOU MOST LIKE?

Use this crazy flowchart to find out!

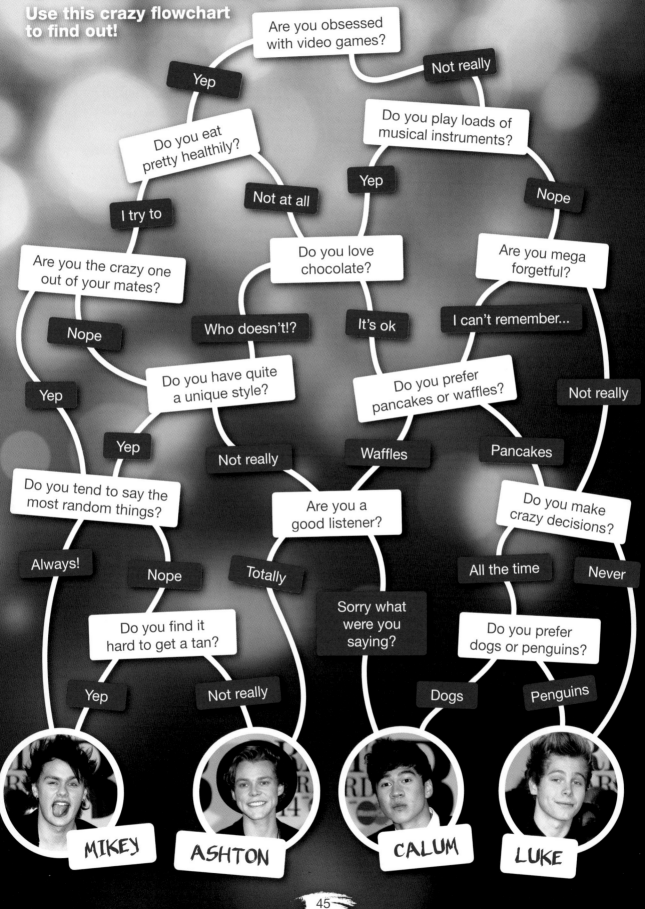

TELL ME A STORY...

We all dream about hanging out with the boys in real life, but have you ever thought about what would actually happen if you did? Imagine you woke up on the 5 Seconds of Summer tour bus. You'll be spending the whole day with them! Write an awesome short story using the following words at least once (plus your own words, duh!):

tour bus - pizza - dancing - guitars - koala - adventure - stage - lyrics - hair dye - socks

THAT MOMENT WHEN...

There's no doubt that 5 Seconds of Summer know how to put on a good show in their music videos. Here are 10 amazing moments from their videos so far. Check out the time given after each one so you can look them up later!

She Looks So Perfect

- When Mikey leaps onto his knees for that amazing guitar solo. YES. (1:09)

- The policeman dancing around in the road in his underwear. Just because. (3:05)

Don't Stop

- When Calum (AKA Cal Pal) looks at the camera and seems on the verge of bursting into giggles. (0:22)

- Luke (AKA Doctor Fluke) getting attacked by an old lady after trying to help her cross the road! (1:31)

- Ashton's (AKA Smash) little victory dance with his stereo. (3:05)

Out Of My Limit

- Luke's crazy smile for a selfie with a lucky fan. (1:45)

- Mikey and Ashton holding wine glasses to their ears. We have no idea why it happens, but it's hilarious. (0:30)

Heartbreak Girl

- The huge leap they take into the air down a quiet little side street. (1:40)

Try Hard

- When Calum sings about his crush being into drummers and Ashton points at himself excitedly, all while zooming about on a roller coaster. (1:30)

- To be honest... any action shot of the boys on the roller coaster. It's 5 Seconds of Summer! Flying through the air at great speed! Singing!

CRISS-CROSS!

Can you fill in this tricky crossword? Hint– most of the answers are scattered throughout the annual – keep your eyes peeled!

ACROSS

4. Calum's superhero name. (3,3)

8. The city of red double-decker buses and Buckingham Palace, where the boys once went on a song-writing trip that would change everything. (6)

9. Luke's superhero name. (6,5)

11. *The Lord of the Rings* was filmed there. There are lots of sheep there. Calum's mum is from there... (3,7)

12. The place where Ashton was born. (7)

DOWN

1. The name of Luke's dog. (5)

2. Michael's superhero name. (10)

3. The jazzy wind instrument played by Ashton. (9)

5. On their 2015 tour, this is what the boys plan to do with their socks out. (4,3)

6. Teenage Mutant Ninja _____ - the guys once dressed up as them and they share a love of pizza. (7)

7. The type of clothing she looks so perfect standing there in. (9)

10. Ashton's superhero name. (5)

If you're really stuck you can check the answers on page 61.

DID YOU KNOW?

Apparently, Michael came up with the name '5 Seconds of Summer' during a maths lesson. Hmm, we wonder what his teacher has to say about that!

Michael loves Cadbury's Twirls.

Ashton used to be in a band called 'Swallow the Goldfish'. Hmm, we hope he didn't actually swallow any goldfish...

FITTEST BOY ON THE PLANET

Each of the lads has won the title 'Fittest Boy on the Planet' at the We Love Pop Awards. Surely they can't all be the fittest boy at the same time?!

Ashton tried out for *The X Factor* back in 2010. What were they THINKING letting him go!?

5 SECONDS OF SUMMER AND ONE DIRECTION: THE BROMANCE

The lovely lads of One Direction gave 5 Seconds of Summer the chance of a lifetime when they asked them to head out on tour with them. Not only did 5 Seconds of Summer learn some valuable lessons about touring the world, but they had an amazing time! What's more... a friendship blossomed between the two bands. This is no normal friendship. It's magical. It's beautiful. It's a bromance!

If you were lucky enough to see any of the shows on the Take Me Home Tour, you probably would have seen all the boys jumping around the stage together and generally having the time of their lives.

Then, there's the backstage antics. There are endless videos online of all the pop rockers playing pranks on each other, chilling out, stuffing their faces and generally being boys (it's all part of the bromance)!

Check out what 5 Seconds of Summer have to say about One Direction:

"They've given us the biggest opportunity of our lives, you know? We're just from my garage in Sydney." - Ashton
(pressparty.com)

"Learning how to tour from the lads really changed our lives."- Calum
(seventeen.com)

"There's usually a lot of fruit throwing! They're really funny guys. Their humour is really similar to ours." - Calum
(seventeen.com)

"We talk the most with Niall—but we get along really well with [all of the guys]." - All the boys
(seventeen.com)

TAKE ME HOME

The boys' tour schedule with One Direction was completely jam-packed! These are just a few of the gigs they played. Can you match the city names up with the country they belong to?

1.	Antwerp	A.	Japan
2.	Milan	B.	Belgium
3.	Lisbon	C.	New Zealand
4.	Montreal	D.	Italy
5.	Seattle	E.	Germany
6.	Auckland	F.	Canada
7.	Brisbane	G.	Portugal
8.	Tokyo	H.	USA
9.	Manchester	I.	Australia
10.	Berlin	J.	England

We've put the answers on page 61.

53

WHAT'S IN A NAME?

Er, quite a lot actually! A name isn't just something for people to call you. It defines your whole identity and can really say a lot about someone's personality. So, let's discover the meaning behind 5 Seconds of Summer's names, and see if they match up with how the boys really are...

LUKE

This name means 'light' or 'of light'. It hails back to a Greek physician who lived in biblical times. He eventually became the patron saint of doctors. This guy started a trend for people with this name being hard-working individuals, who study hard. Lukes are dependable, thoughtful sorts who are easy to rely on. Their intelligence, charm and confidence often makes them irresistible and comforting to be around. These all sound like great characteristics for the frontman of such a huge band! Possibly the most attractive trait about Lukes is that they never try too hard to get attention (we guess the lyrics in Try Hard couldn't have been about Luke then), so they actually end up receiving it anyway!

ASHTON

Ashton has only started being used as a first name in the last three hundred years, it was actually more popular as a surname. It comes from the old English meaning 'Ash Tree'. Cool! Ashtons love their freedom, and are always on the search for adventure. They're often quite intellectual too, and like to learn new things every day (hence those awesome drumming skills). People with this name are good at adapting to whatever situation they end up in, and they always maintain an easy-going outlook on life. This means they're great at looking on the bright side... which explains Ashton's permanent cheeky grin!

MICHAEL

Also a biblical name, Michael started being used in the western world in the 12th century. They are affectionate, compassionate people who like to take care of others. They worry and fuss a lot about their family and friends and are happy when everyone just gets along! Michaels can also be very sensitive, so they need lots of affection themselves too. The fact that Michaels care a lot about other people means they are natural teachers who constantly try to help others improve. They're also very hard working though, and often end up being very successful without even trying! They will always handle this success well, as they're very grounded individuals. Well, Michael is certainly good at 'keeping it real', don't you think?

CALUM

This is a Scottish name (Calum has a Scottish dad) that comes from Saint Columba, who was pretty much the Scottish version of Ireland's Saint Patrick. Columba is Latin, and means 'dove'. Calums usually achieve a lot in life, and this is because they're great at problem-solving. Their intelligence leads to them doing well in many different areas, though they always remain humble. That definitely sounds like the Calum we know! Calums only ever really appreciate success if they've stayed true to themselves. These guys are also quite tough, and dedicated to getting what they want out of situations. They often end up in great positions of power, but their sense of humour and general friendliness means that they never come across as intimidating (in fact, quite the opposite). We couldn't imagine our Calum hurting a fly, so this definitely sounds about right!

A FEW OF THEIR FAVOURITE THINGS...

Raindrops on roses and whiskers on kittens? Um, probably not. The guys' favourite things are a little bit more rock 'n' roll than that! Or are they..?

Luke loves...
- The beach.
- *How I Met Your Mother*.
- Cookies & Cream ice cream... yum!
- *Take Off Your Pants and Jacket*, an album by Blink-182, one of his fave bands.
- Mila Kunis – celeb crush alert!
- Ham and cheese (random).

Michael loves...
- The word 'cheeseburger'. Fair enough.
- Watermelon bubblegum.
- Long walks.
- All hair colours (you don't say!)
- Spider-Man.
- Gaming.

Ashton loves...

- *Family Guy*.
- Heavy music...
- ...but also John Mayer!
- Banana milkshakes.
- Vans shoes.
- Caramel Koalas (an Aussie chocolate bar!)

Calum loves...

- R 'n' B music - no way!
- Katy Perry (another celeb crush!)
- Going to the gym.
- Ham and pineapple pizza (that explains the need for the gym).
- Playing soccer.
- Happy Meals (he clearly must spend a lot of time in the gym).

R'n'B

And all the boys love... their FANS! Erm, that's YOU.

ANSWERS

SPOT THE DIFFERENCE (PAGE 22)

THE BEST 5 SECONDS OF SUMMER QUIZ... EVER! (PAGE 24)

1. 2011 of course!
2. *Please Don't Go* by Mike Posner.
3. Ashton! He went to Richmond High School.
4. A dog! Ketchup is a cute white plastic dog the boys found in a house they stayed at in LA. So cute!
5. To win the 5 Seconds of Summer ice-cream eating competition, of course!
6. Michael! Hmm, we wonder if all that Manga watching is what inspired that big hair...
7. The Cronulla Sharks.
8. Vegemite! Mmm, delicious.
9. Good Charlotte! Joel and Benji Madden have since formed a band called The Madden Brothers – so we'll give you that one if that was your answer!
10. Calum! AKA, Cal-Pal.
11. A penguin! His profile name is 'luke_is_a_penguin'. Random.
12. Calum! Och aye.
13. Blonde! We heart his ever-changing rainbow hair though.
14. Take Me Home.
15. 2013. Good work boys!
16. Calum, he almost played for Australia!
17. *Amnesia*! Ooft, that was a tricky one.
18. Rock! We hope you didn't say 'boy'.
19. Ashton! Well, we do hear they're very comfy!
20. Michael. What a lucky guy! Ronnie that is.

WORD UP! (PAGE 30)

Mike-Ro-Wave was hiding in the wordsearch! Did you spot him?

```
K P U N K R P K L E X T
B T B T A K Q A T M P H
M V R T X R T I Z T I V
W I I U E K M L Y Y H O
Z U K M O E D A L L S C
G B M E G T G R F Q D A
M U A E R Q J T X H N L
S J V S M O R S P T E S
J K V D S O W U Z W I B
K F R A C S D A E H R R
Z M T K X H W D V R F M
K N D R U M S M N E K X
```

ALL MUDDLED UP! (PAGE 31)

1. Don't Stop
2. English Love Affair
3. Good Girls
4. Long Way Home
5. She Looks So Perfect

TRUE OR FALSE? (PAGE 31)

1. False! It was Louis Tomlinson.
2. True! Can't say we blame him.
3. True! Good taste Ashton, good taste.
4. False! That would be awesome though wouldn't it?
5. False! Don't tell us you fell for that one!

CRISS-CROSS (PAGE 48)

TAKE ME HOME (PAGE 53)

1. Antwerp, Belgium
2. Milan, Italy
3. Lisbon, Portugal
4. Montreal, Canada
5. Seattle, USA
6. Auckland, New Zealand
7. Brisbane, Australia
8. Tokyo, Japan
9. Manchester, England
10. Berlin, Germany

WHERE ARE 5 SECONDS OF SUMMER?

Pur-lease. We are such big fans, we would be able to spot 5 Seconds of Summer a mile away. They're right th...- oh. Wait. What. Where did they go? We lost them! HELP! Can you spot them in the crowd?